Wisps & Wafts of a Wayfaring Wanderer

AF624560

Philllip Compton

BookLeaf Publishing

Presentation by *BookLeaf Publishing*

Web: www.bookleafpub.com

E-mail: info@bookleafpub.com

ISBN: 9789357212540

First edition 2023

This book is dedicated to my wife -- my best friend & the love of my life -- Cynthia Compton. Such a small tribute pales in comparison to all that she's brought to my life.

ACKNOWLEDGEMENT

Thanks to all those who've inspired in me vision and sparked my imagination over the course of my life, and those who've given to me a love and appreciation for the English language. These are, of course, too numerous to mention, but the first that comes to mind is my high school sophomore English teacher -- Ms. Ruth Lewis. She challenged me beyond what I would have ever pursued on my own, and for that she has my everlasting gratitude. Her faith in me affected in me a self-confidence and faith in myself during a very formative time in my life. Thank you for believing in me more than I've ever believed in myself. I still think of you every time I smell grape bubble gum.

And then there was the tall, thin, librarian-like lady that I once talked to in the miniature store on a back road near Magic World in Pigeon Forge, TN. One day, when I was maybe ten or twelve years old, I was out riding my bike and wandered into the shop on a whim, and mostly because I'd never been in there before. Making small talk with the only other person in the shop, she scolded me for watching a movie when there was a book available for the story. I left thinking about what an unpleasant encounter that was, but remembered it over the years, and the lesson stuck -- and today I owe her a massive debt of gratitude for taking the time to fuss at a little boy who'd stopped by her shop that was too lazy to read when he could just watch the movie.

I also wish to thank those who've served as sounding boards and provide feedback for my works -- Cynthia Compton, Dylan Walsh, Sherry Smith, Trenton Chestnut, Randy Compton, Tommy Roberts, Shannon McLeod, Tom Thorne, Mary Tipton, and a bunch of others that I'm forgetting but should be including here.

I also want to thank the late Frank Bray for his enthusiasm and encourage for whatever endeavor I'd undertaken. He would've loved this and been right in the middle of it -- you can't imagine how much I wish you were here, buddy! We love & miss you greatly!

Lastly, I'd like to include everyone that knows what an Oxford comma is and who uses it properly.

THANK YOU!!

PREFACE

This little book is as much light reading material destined for the back of a toilet as it is a glimpse into the things that pervade my very consciousness. The poems found herein are just as light or as heavy -- as superficial or as deep -- as you want them to be.

Join this rookie author as I take my first turn at bat. It is for you, the reader, to decide whether I have hit a homerun or struck out. Be gentle.

Marriage Counseling Gone Wrong

For twenty-five years,
they shared the same life --
Two and a half decades
as husband and wife.

She sought marriage counseling,
so they might get along --
As a couple, she wanted
their bond to be strong.

The counselor asked them,
"What brings you here?
Now, what are the problems,
just so we're clear?"

The wife who'd sat quietly
took that as her cue,
To recount her grievances,
which were quite a few.

She complained of this
and complained of that,
While her husband beside her
in silence sat.

She felt neglected
    and empty inside,
Unloved and unwanted
    most of the time.

There was no intimacy,
    she felt all alone.
Her list of complaints
    seemed to be a mile long.

On she rambled,
    back to the day they were wed,
Quoting their vows,
    word-for-word what was said.

Her tirade she kept up
    for quite awhile.
The therapist just sat back,
    listened, and smiled.

Having heard enough,
    the counselor did rise,
Walked to the woman,
    and looked in her eyes.

Without a word,
    he swept up her hand,
Bowed at the waist,
    and asked her to stand.

The therapist took her
    in his embrace,
As a look of shock
    appeared on her face.

He kissed her with passion
    that she'd never known,
And when he'd finished,
    her strength was all gone.

Back into her chair
    she fell in a daze,
While her husband just watched
    with one eyebrow raised.

The counselor said to the man,
    "For this to succeed,
At least three times a week,
    this is what your wife needs.

It will surely give
    your marriage advantage.
Is this something that
    you think you can manage?"

He replied, "Mondays and Wednesdays
    I can do as you wish,
But I can't drop her off Friday,
    because on Friday I fish."

In Need of a Push

Awakened in the morning
   at a quarter 'til three,
From a deep, peaceful sleep
   and dreams not to be.

A loud pounding they heard
   on the front door,
The wife sent her husband
   to find out what for.

She pulled up the covers
   around her chin
And waited for him
   to return again.

He headed downstairs
   with a baseball bat,
Ready for trouble,
   if it came to that.

Standing in the rain
   just outside the front door,
Soaked to the bone
   and sloshed to the core,

Was a poor, drunken soul
    who spoke with a slur,
Oblivious to time
    and rain, as it were,

"Friend, could you give
    a fellow a push?"
He staggered
    and almost fell on his tush.

"If you could help me,
    it would sure mean a lot!"
The man said, "Get off my lawn,
    you pathetic sot.

Yes, it's help that you need,
    but not help from me --
What you need's a cold shower
    and some strong, black coffee."

The drunkard persisted,
    not accepting a 'shush,'
"Please, sir, just someone
    to give me a push."

"No!" the man yelled,
    "Get out of my yard,"
As he turned back inside
    and slammed the door hard.

Back upstairs, his wife asked,
"Who was it, dear?"
"Just some bloke who's drunk
way too much beer.

He needed a push --
I guess he broke down."
"Well, did you help him,"
his wife asked with a frown.

"Of course not," he said,
"It's the middle of the night,
And on top of that,
the weather's afright!"

She said "Have you forgotten
that we've been in his shoes?
It's not been three months
since we needed pushed, too.

At the mercy of strangers,
someone helped us with that,
Even though he didn't know us
from Adam's house cat.

When we broke down
on the other side of town,
Of all the people we knew,
none could be found.

So never mind the rain --
    go back and help him,
Just as we got helped
    when we were out on a limb.

He sighed as he bent down
    and put on his shoes.
This was an argument
    that he knew he would lose.

He stepped outside
    and called out quite loudly,
"Hey, buddy, do you still need
    that push from me?".

Dark it was,
    and the rain didn't help any,
But he could hear the voice slur,
    "Yes, sir, please!"

He yelled, "Where you at?
    I can't see a thing!"
The drunk hollered back,
    "I'm over here -- on the swing!

Ticket to Ride

Gathered at the station,
    Fixin' to board a train,
They chose this mode of travel,
    over car, bus, or plane.

They waited to buy tickets
    at windows, side-by-side,
Three boys from a nearby city,
    three from the countryside.

To the same conference,
    Traveling the same way,
And as fate would have it,
    the same train and same day.

The three city boys
    each bought the ticket they'd need,
While the country boys bought
    one ticket for all three.

The city boys made fun of them,
    laughing behind their backs.
When behind their backs got old,
    They smirked, "Hey, Crackerjacks!"

"Don't you hillbillies know
    you need a ticket apiece?
In case you can't count,
    that would be three -- capiche?"

(The hillbillies must've felt
    especially gracious that day,
'Cause the city boys got to keep their teeth
    and were able to walk away.)

Those boys from the backwoods
    just smiled and said with a wink,
"You think you're so smart, watch this,
    then see what you think."

The three city boys went on ahead,
    for the train to board,
Then waited for those from the hills,
    who had to be out of their gourds.

Finally, they came on board,
    but not to sit down.
On to the bathroom small,
    which they directly found.

They piled into the room,
    although not with ease,
Then they heard the conductor's
    cry, "Ticket, please!"

The city dwellers just proffered
    their tickets and grinned,
Keeping an eye on the bathroom
    that hid their new-found friends.

At the trio's cramped hideout,
    the conductor finally arrived,
playing into the plan
    that the three of them contrived.

"Ticket, please,"
    he said as he knocked,
Patiently waiting
    while the latch came unlocked.

The door opened a crack,
    and a hand did appear,
Holding the one ticket --
    those watching saw it clear.

Satisfied, the ticket
    collector moved on,
Then the three reemerged
    once they knew that he was gone.

They took their place in their seats,
    very much amused
The city boys were impressed
    with their little ruse.

"Hey, we should try that
    going back," one said --
And once it was heard,
    the thought stuck in their heads.

So quickly was it decided,
    they'd buy one instead of three.
The good ol' boys just sat back,
    listening to their strategy.

Then when the conference was over,
    and it was time for them to leave,
They gathered back at the station,
    grinning like they were thieves.

The city boys at the window
    bought their single ticket,
But the thing that they saw next, --
    they just could not believe it!

The hillbillies just sat there
    and never got in line.
No ticket did they purchase,
    yet everything seemed fine.

The city slickers said,
    "There's just no way!
You simply cannot ride
    unless one of you pays!"

The good ol' boys were
    each holding back a grin.
"Watch and learn," they said,
    to the dandies' chagrin.

The country boys boarded
    and found their hideaway.
The others found another bathroom,
    just across the hallway.

When they were there,
    hidden in their places,
A hillbilly poked his head out
    sure to look both ways,

Then went to the bathroom
    where the others were squeezed,
Knocked on the door
    and said, "Ticket, please!"

One More Chance

Eighty thousand blondes,
    together one and all --
Were gathered in a stadium,
    standing proud and tall.

"Blondes ain't that dumb,"
    they want the world to know,
United in a common cause,
    to prove that it is so.

A man on a stage
    called a blonde lady from the crowd,
Cameras flashed and folks cheered
    as she made her way down.

In front of a microphone
    and several TV cameras,
The host said, "You guys have got this.
    You're like samurais!"

A cheer went up,
    and when it finally died down,
The chosen one was standing there,
    sporting the smile of a clown.

"We're about to prove
that blondes ain't that dumb,
Here's how this will work,
along with the outcome.

I'll ask a question
that you're gonna answer,
To show that you're fit
to be more than a dancer.

Your mental prowess
for the world to see,
They'll know being blonde
doesn't make one a dummy!"

The blonde just squared
her shoulders and nodded,
The crowd grew quiet,
after they'd applauded.

When he saw she was ready,
thus began the emcee,
"Your question, my dear --
what's twenty plus twenty?"

She thought and she pondered,
you could see her gears turning,
Thinking all the way back
to her grade school learning,

She spoke into the mic
    when she finally said,
"Is it thirty-two?"
    And the host just shook his head.

"No, I'm afraid that
    'thirty-two' is not correct --
'Forty' was the answer
    that we would expect."

The crowd began to chant,
    as if in a trance,
"Give her another chance!
    Give her another chance!"

When the cries died down
    and the host could speak,
His contestant beside him
    all sheepish and meek,

He said, "Well, I guess we could,
    as there's really no rules,
Just some questions to separate
    the sages from the fools."

To the blonde he asked,
    "Would you like to try again?"
Then the crowd erupted,
    and went totally insane.

"Okay, okay! Quiet!
    Settle down, please," yelled he.
Then, "Your next question is this --
    what is ten plus three?"

"Take your time," he said
    when he heard her whine.
She shut her eyes, then finally asked,
    "Is it twenty-nine?"

He hesitated, while the crowd
    held their breath as one.
"No, that's not right.
    I'm afraid that now we are done."

"Give her another chance,"
    came the mantra once more,
As they chanted and clapped
    and stomped their feet on the floor.

"We do have
    eighty thousand of you here --
Blondes gathered
    from afar and from near."

"One last question we'll have --
    we're all pulling for you!
And this will be your problem, dear,
    what is two plus two?"

She thought about it long and hard,
    looking at the floor,
Then stepped up to the mic and said,
    "The answer's four."

Before the emcee could
    confirm or deny,
Pandemonium ensued
    as the crowd went wild.

Eighty thousand strong
    jumped to their feet,
All stomping and clapping,
    as they picked up the beat,

Louder the chant resumed,
    as if all were back in a trance --
"Give her another chance!
    Give her another chance!"

Slow Poke: A Fable in Meter

There once was a cowboy whose horse wouldn't gallop --
It barely could manage a trot.
When gathered with others at the local saloon,
He was always a laughing stock.

He'd poke & he'd prod & goad the horse on,
And call it all manner of names,
But no matter what he said or he did,
The results were always the same.

The horse would balk and slow down his gait
And refuse to pick up the pace.
The slower he'd go, the more the man cussed
And pleaded and begged and prayed.

He thought and he pondered and made up his mind --
He knew what he had to do.
The cowboy smiled as he began to envision
A bottle of Elmer's glue.

"Git it t'gether," He said to the horse,
"or here's what'll happen to you..." --
"I found a fact'ry that'll pay me good money,
They wanna boil you down into goo."

The horse gulped hard and his eyes got big
As he stood & pondered his fate.
He'd have to get rid of his stubborn streak
And quick -- before it's too late!

He tried to gallop and gave it his all,
And did his dead level best,
But all he could manage was the same as before
--
He never would pass the test.

"Let's go to town," the farmer said to his horse,
Who began to tremble with fear.
"This must be the day," the horse thought to
himself,
"My end is drawing near!"

With courage he went, resigned to his fate,
Walking tall & standing proud.
He refused to let his worries show,
He'd meet his Maker without a sound.

On the way to town by the neighbor's farm,
The horse couldn't believe his eyes --
'Twas the most beautiful mare that he'd ever
seen,
Walking along the fence by his side.

She gave him a glance, a whinny, & neigh,
Then took off in a full-blown sprint.
To the cowboy's surprise, his horse gave chase,
Following her as she went.

The cowboy yelled, "Whoa," and jerked up on the reins,
And damned the poor horse to hell,
But he didn't slow down until the end of the fence,
Where the mare had stopped as well.

The horse put on the brakes and came to a stop,
Which took his rider by surprise --
The cowboy yelled as momentum took over,
And he left his saddle behind.

Over the fence, the horses gazed at each other,
Then turned to take in the sight.
They'd never seen such in all of their days --
Cowboys weren't made to fly!

The cow poke got up and dusted his chaps
And looked at the horses and sighed.
He looked himself over and picked up his hat --
All that seemed to be broke was his pride.

He climbed on his horse and spurred him good
And turned up the drive to his neighbor's.
He found him hard at work in the barn
And asked him to rest from his labors.

He was looking to trade and would make him a deal,
If he'd just take the horse off his hands
The horse would be happy to make his home here,
But he was more than the cowboy could stand.

His heart leapt within him at the joy that he felt,
When the horse heard what the cowboy had said,
The neighbor just smiled, pushed back his hat,
And commenced to scratching his head.

"Now what would I do with a horse like that,"
The neighbor asked as he considered the trade.
The mare trotted up to the neighbor's side,
Bowed her head, pawed the ground, and neighed.

"Well, I guess I could always use a good stud,
If you think a stud he would make."
Upon hearing this, the horse perked up his ears,
Then fainted dead away.

Upon waking, he found himself living a dream,
More than he'd ever hoped.
The grass was indeed greener on the other side,
Contrary to what he'd been told.

If you ever get cussed for doing your job too slow
Or threatened to be made into glue,
Find a sweet philly and win her heart true,
And this might even happen to you!

A Dog Who Could Talk

A man I knew had a dog that could talk.
Every day he'd take it out for a walk.
Tell his business, it would,
To all that it could,
But most people would just stand there & gawk.

To town the man went, a muzzle he bought,
Put it on his pup, & the lesson was taught.
But the dog, you see,
Could also read --
The lesson was not as taught as he thought.

The instructions it read, both front & back,
But opposable thumbs was something it lacked.
Try as it might,
The latch was too tight,
The puppy gave up, for it knew it was trapped.

Quiet it was, without the mutt's chatter,
And the man found he missed the dog's endless pratter.
So quiet in fact,
The man's nerves were wracked,
To always be thinking about such a matter.

Finally one day, after ages it seems,
The man took the muzzle, & the dog was relieved.
His tail he did wag,
His butt he did drag,
To show to his master how much he was pleased.

The dog was delighted to do the man's bidding,
And now he knew that the man wasn't kidding.
Be quiet, he must,
To earn the man's trust,
Because talking by him was clearly forbidden.

He woofed, barked, & yelped, & make no mistake --
He made all the sounds that a good dog would make.
He yipped & he growled,
And he yapped & he howled,
But not a word would he utter, to the poor man's dismay.

To please his human, the dog devoted his life,
To obey his commands and avoid any strife.
But no orders he gave
For the dog to obey,
Except for the occasional "Speak!" or the like.

Upon that command, he'd bark his best,
Sometimes with a growl from deep in his chest.
A dejected sigh,
A half-hearted smile,
Was proof that his human was surely impressed.

And never again for all of his days --
Not one single word would the gifted dog say.
Silent but true,
He knew what to do --
Devoted and faithful, by the man's side he'd stay.

The Crooked Man's Fate

There once lived a gambler,
A restless rambler,
Who never knew how much to bet.
For each time he gambled,
It all turned to shambles,
And he found himself deeper in debt.

Only one thing was certain,
He'd come out a-hurtin',
And you could take that to the bank.
The outcome was sure,
His loss he'd endure --
A failure was he, if you want to be frank.

Now a good gambler can
Devise such a plan
That will cost you all of your wealth,
If you take your loss
And consider the cost,
You might get away with your health.

So it happened one day
While in search of a game
Where he might turn an ante or three,
That he happened upon

A man that seemed stoned,
That appeared just as unlucky as he.

'Twas the mark that he sought,
Or so he had thought,
Where he might score himself a quick purse.
Finding someone to play
Was not his forte,
And his foresight could not have been worse.

Said the gambler, "I'm Scott,
And I'll tell you what --
I've got a good game we can play.
So give it a chance,
And your circumstance
Is bound to improve this day."

The man said, "I'm Ben,
And I reckon I'm in,
But the wager will have to stay modest.
I don't have a lot
To put in the pot,
'Cause I'm broke, to be perfectly honest."

Scott said, "That'll be fine,
Just put up your dime,
And this game we'll play, if you're able.
We'll both lay a bet,
And the winner will get
All that's been put on the table."

"Well, it sounds good to me,"
Ben said with some glee,
As he proffered a dime for his stake.
"But I don't understand
Who'll win the first hand --
But I must before a bet I'll make."

"It's easy as pie!"
Scott's grin turned wry.
"I'll explain it all, just trust me.
The rules to this game
Are always the same,
It's really quite simple -- you'll see."

"We both draw a card --
See, it isn't that hard!
If they match, then the winner I'm crowned.
But should they be diff'rent,
Well, then we consent,
That you've certainly lost that round."

"Well, I guess that'll work,"
Ben said with a smirk,
And 'fore they knew it, it was well underway.
Ben lost the first few,
As we'd expect him to do,
Then kept losing as his bank dwindled away.

Then a shift of fate --
I cannot relate
What happened in their contest that day.
Lady Luck frowned
Upon the one crowned
To win all the games that they played.

Scott took a beatin' --
Which meant someone's cheatin'.
And his ears turned red, as they do when he's
mad,
Then he ranted and raved,
And called Ben a knave,
For he'd taken the last penny Scott had.

Scott called him out,
Without any doubt,
"I've caught you now, for Scott's not my real
name!
I'm Ricky the Rambler,
The riverboat gambler,
And there's no way you've won all those games."

"That's fine," said Ben,
With an ear-to-ear grin,
"My last name's Dover, so be it what may --
I'm Karma incarnate,
You've met your own Fate,
'Cause I've come to settle with you today."

So if you're a lout
That goes about
Ripping off those who'll play a fixed game,
Before it's all done,
And you've had your fun,
A visit from Ben might just bring you to shame.

~~~~~~~~~~~~~~~~~~~~~~~

One fateful day, when your time has come,
Then it will all be over...
When Karma comes, and your luck runs dumb,
You'll be introduced to Ben Dover!

If you're lucky, he'll leave you with nothing to show.
If not, you'll be deep in debt.
Your motives determine just how it'll go, but it's a lesson you won't soon forget!!
~~~~~~~~~~~~~~~~~~~~~~~

Ballad of Charlie and Adeline

Ballad of Charlie and Adeline (and Willie the Whopper)

Charlie was a gunfighter
  in the old West,
They say none was better --
  he was the best.

He never missed with his .44,
  his aim was quick and true.
Yet never had he shot a man,
  nor had he reason to.

He struck fear in the hearts
  of those he shot at most --
Whether it was targets on boards
  or bottles sitting on posts.

A restless spirit he had,
  wanderlust in his soul,
With the wind as his guide,
  where it blew, he would go.

He traveled the land,
  never settled down --
He just drifted and wandered
  from town to town.

He'd do odd jobs
  for the people he'd meet.
A carpenter, a mason,
  a blacksmith was he.

I guess you could say
  he was a jack-of-all-trades,
And after living expenses,
  he still had it made.

Carefree and fearless
  was he most of the time,
'Til the day that he met
  pretty Adeline.

She spoke in a whisper,
  so soft and so low,
That it melted his heart,
  like the sun melts the snow.

She more glided than walked,
  so graceful was she,
When she crossed a room,
  it was something to see.

Everyone knew
  that she'd make quite the wife
For the fortunate suitor
  who would pledge her his life.

Cupid's arrow must
  have been true in its flight,
'Cause when Charlie saw her,
  it was love at first sight.

He sought her affection,
  her heart for to win,
And determined to woo her
  until she gave in.

But there was a problem
  with the courtship he'd planned,
She belonged to another,
  who'd not understand.

He was twice her age,
  and had been promised her hand,
An arranged marriage
  to one from the homeland.

Although William was
  her betrothed's given name proper,
Most that knew him just called him
  Willie the Whopper --

Though not to his face
  they referred to him thus,
For when he would hear it,
  he'd raise Cain and cuss.

Now William was a big man
  and round as a barrel,
But to anger him such
  would put you in peril.

His temper would flare,
  and his fists would lash out,
Some unlucky soul'd
  take a beating, no doubt.

Charlie heard rumors
  that his quest was in vain,
That Willie would put him
  in a world of pain.

Charlie, he was never afeared,
  and his resolve, it never faltered.
He'd continue in his lovelorn pursuit,
  until the day that he finally caught her.

When Willie had heard
  what Charlie was thinking,
He went to the bar
  and commenced to drinking.

'Twas just a matter of time
  'til that Charlie stopped by,
But by then, Willie'd
  drunk himself cross-eyed.

Willie jumped to his feet
  and then started to strut,
Tripped over his chair,
  and fell on his butt.

He grabbed hold of a table
  to get up to his feet,
Much to the dismay
  of those trying to eat.

The table upended,
  food flying about,
And four angry diners
  about to freak out.

Willie struggled,
  pulling himself to one knee,
Wearing chicken marsala
  and a glass of Chablis.

Charlie just watched
  and held back a grin,
As the big man slipped
  and fell down again.

This time he took with him
  a full game of poker
Leaving stuck to his forehead
  an ace and a joker.

Cards and money
  about him were scattered,
Shot glasses, whiskey,
  and a bottle that shattered.

Distracted by trying
  to get to his feet,
Willie didn't notice
  Adeline so sweet

As she slipped right on through
  the two swinging doors,
Past the patrons who were watching
  the show on the floor,

Right on up to Charlie,
  who leaned on the bar,
Watching the spectacle,
  safe from afar.

Climbing a spectator
  who was standing close by,
Willie got to his feet,
  one hand on his thigh.

Straightening himself up
  and looking 'round the room,
His eyes fell on Charlie,
  then the whole show resumed.

With a big hand he pointed
  straight at his prey,
Then took a step toward him,
  teeth clenched with rage.

So focused was Willie
  upon his next victim,
Or perhaps 'twas the booze
  that caused him to miss 'em,

But the diners and gamblers
  whose tables he'd flipped,
Were forming a mob --
  and he was about to be whipped.

"We've had quite enough
  of your bullying ways,
It's high time that somebody
  put you in your place!

With your crap we're fed up
  and with having to cope --
We'll find a tall tree
  and short piece of rope..."

But that thought they
  were not able to finish --
Their bravado all
  of a sudden diminished,

When the shot rang out
  from a .44 pistol,
And the words that followed
  were as clear as a crystal.

Everyone turned toward him
  as the smoke cleared,
Toward ol' Charlie, who'd just
  ordered a beer.

There by Adeline,
  mighty tall did he stand,
One arm 'round her waist,
  and six-gun in hand.

He said, "There will be
  no lynching today.
This'll be resolved
  a far better way."

William's sins all've been
  misdeeds of the past,
Except for tonight,
  when he whooped his own ass.

But that was the liquor,
  he meant you no harm.
He simply failed to display
  his usual charm.

Ain't that right, William --
  just nod and say yes."
Which he did in spite
  of all of the mess.

"Now if it'll satisfy
  all you good folks,
William's just leaving town,
  now, ain't you, bloke?

He'll not show his face
  around here again,
If you allow him to leave
  and forgive him his sins."

Willie just nodded
  and walked up to the man,
And, holding his hat,
  he shook Charlie's hand.

As Willie left, Charlie said,
  "Go in peace, friend!
But I'll kill you myself
  if you come here again."

Willie nodded and turned,
his head hung in shame,
But stopped at the door,
half-turned, and exclaimed,

"You're the bigger man than I,
that's obvious to see.
Treat her like the queen that she is, sir,
And happy I know you'll both be."

Willie left that day, and in those parts
never again was he seen.
Some say he was found in the desert
with a bone-dry canteen.

Others say he lived out his days
plagued with some rare disorder.
A few say a cute señorita
lured him south of the border.

We'll probably never learn
of poor Willie's fate,
But Charlie and Adeline --
they just couldn't wait.

They were wed by a preacher
on the very next day,
For none thought of a reason
why they should delay.

The exploits of Charlie and Adeline,
  we could go on to tell,
But those are best left for another time,
  for another teller to tell.

Boyhood Imaginings

A stick for a sword,
    imaginary shield
And armor -- oh,
    how I wish they were real!

I'm off on a quest,
    fraught with peril, no doubt,
So I kneel for a prayer
    before I set out.

"Lord, please bless
    your humble servant this day,
Keep me safe always,
    and guard my way.

As I venture forth
    into unknown domains.
May I bring you glory
    and honor, I pray."

In the garage where I stable
    my trusted mount --
We've been on more trips
    than I can count --

Donning my helm,
    I climb on my steed.
Rugged and stalwart,
    and unmatched for speed

He flies like the wind --
    on him do I ride.
Huffy's his name,
    written there on his side.

A hearty "Tally ho,"
    and on the road are we,
In search of our fortune,
    wherever it be --

Down the road or up
    some forgotten trail,
Ready for adventure,
    and all that entails.

We ride on and wonder
    what wonders await.
We're coming prepared
    to meet now our fates.

~~~~~~~~~~~~~~~~~~~~~~~~~~~~

Up ahead is a clearing
    in this enchanted backwood,
~~~~~~~~~~~~~~~~~~~~~~~~~~~~

First bit of sky we've seen,
since back in my neighborhood.

What will we find there?
What will appear?
My heart skips a beat
as we draw near.

We've finally made it
to the edge of the wood,
And it's too late to turn back --
but not that we would.

For she's already seen us,
looking up from her chore,
There's no escape now,
But what were we hoping for?

Stooped over is she,
there with a black feline,
Before her a basket
and clothes hung on twine.

I brace myself up
and steady my nerves.
I tell myself,
"It could always be worse!"

Just then she yells,
    "What are you doing there?"
I try to speak,
    but just stutter and stammer.

She must be a witch,
    that's plain to see,
And an evil one, too --
    maybe a banshee!

Out gathering toadstools
    for some wicked spell,
Or beetles and bugs,
    I can't really tell!

Would she turn me
    into a frog today,
Or something worse --
    it's hard to say!

I look around
    to find a way out,
But none could I see,
    though I look all about.

Opposite me in the clearing
    was her abode,
And I know beyond that,
    there must be a road.

To my right there's a fence
    all along the glen,
But to the left... to the left
    another trail opens!

There she stands,
    wagging her finger,
I don't dare tarry --
    there's no time to linger.

I spur Huffy on,
    to where she stands in her gown,
Then hit the brakes hard
    & lay Huffy down,

Dirt fills the air,
    going everywhere,
All in her basket,
    and all in her hair.

She waves her arms 'round,
    and screams words I don't know,
Towards the new trail we fly --
    it's time that we go!

I look back & see
    the witch as I fled,
Try to kick her basket,
    but fall in it instead.

More words she yells,
    as I ride away,
Mostly ones
    I'm not allowed to say.

~~~~~~~~~~~~~~~~~~~~~~~~

On through the forest
    we make our way,
My faithful steed and I,
    come what may.

It doesn't take long
    'til the trees again part,
giving way to the sky,
    like a fine work of art.

I pull up abruptly,
    and Huffy, he stops.
We survey the scene
    with all of its props.

But the biggest,
    meanest-looking thing there
Was a huge yellow dragon,
    head way up in the air.
~~~~~~~~~~~~~~~~~~~~~~~~

He's kneeling down,
    which makes his feet look funny,
Like the track on a tank,
    and his hide colored sunny.

He makes popping noises
    and growls and moans,
Along with the most mournful
    and dreadful of groans.

Most of his head is mouth,
    and that mostly teeth,
He swings his neck 'round,
    for a glimpse of me.

What a strange name
    for a dragon is his,
But strange or not,
    there in writing it is...

Tattooed in letters
    at least a foot wide,
It says "Caterpillar"
    on his neck and one side.

He digs a mouthful
    of dirt at a time,
Whatever he's lost,
    I sure hope he finds.

Now that the dust settles,
    and all the smoke's cleared,
I see a thing so awful,
    it can only cause fear.

There in the see-through
    belly of the beast,
Sits a fully grown man,
    probably the dragon's last feast.

Frantic he seems
    as he points straight at me,
Waving his arms
    like he wants me to leave,

"Be brave, gallant soul!"
    I yell back at him,
His situation grave --
    his chances are slim.

"Never fear, for I'll heed
    the warnings you've braved,
Your life's not in vain,
    for another you've saved!"

I bow my head to offer
    a prayer for the doomed.
"Please, Father, make it quick --
    he's Yours I presume.

Don't let him suffer --
hasten his spirit to You."
I close with an "Amen,"
And wave to the man, thank you.

I wipe a tear from my eye
as we turn to go,
It took such courage
to warn me so!

~~~~~~~~~~~~~~~~~~~~~~~~~~~~~~~

We go back through the forest,
the way that we came,
Still seeking and searching
for our fortune and fame.

From beyond the treeline,
What's that I hear?
It's the cry of a maiden --
That much is clear!

I turn Huffy sharp
and cut through the trees,
Across the ditch,
and into the street.
~~~~~~~~~~~~~~~~~~~~~~~~~~~~~~~

The little girl that lives
    three or four houses down
Seems to be the source
    of that disparaging sound.

"How may I assist you,
    Milady so fair?"
She stops her wailing,
    turns and just stares.

For a moment she just
    ogles me up & now down,
As if I was in the circus,
    like some kind of clown.

Finally she sniffles
    and wipes her nose with one hand,
Points with the other
    up the tree where I stand.

I look up to see
    a cat on a limb,
And ask her if she'd like
    for me to get him.

She just nods yes,
    as she wipes away tears.
So I start to climb,
    despite all my fears.

Just as I reach the poor,
    desperate kittycat,
It launches itself like
    a demon-possessed wombat

And lands on my back,
    then claws its way past me,
On down the trunk,
    then off of the tree,

Into the girl's arms
    who is hugging it tight
And breaks into giggles
    with all of her might.

I climb down the tree,
    my back clawed to shreds,
She doesn't say, "Thank you,"
    sticks her tongue out instead.

"Boys have got cooties!
    Get away from me! Go!"
/sigh/ It's not always easy
    being the hero!

From down on the corner,
    I hear ringing bells
A familiar sound,
    and one I know well.

When the church bells ring,
    each night around six,
It's time to go home,
    lickety-split.

For Mom will have cooked
    and supper's on the table.
I must be washed up,
    if I'm at all able.

~~~~~~~~~~~~~~~~~~~~~~~~~~~~

I climb on Huffy
    and get on the road.
As we near my house,
    Huffy, he slows.

Around the city's
    orange construction cones,
Past three driveways,
    and across the lawn.

Finally back home,
    I put Huffy up,
Leave my helmet with him,
    and go in to sup.
~~~~~~~~~~~~~~~~~~~~~~~~~~~~

I stop in the kitchen
    to give Mom a kiss,
She's just finished supper --
    its aroma, pure bliss!

Meatloaf, green beans,
    corn, mashed potatoes,
Dinner rolls, iced tea --
    pretty good as it goes!

I go wash today
    off my hands and my face,
Find my place at the table,
    and then say grace.

I recount and tell
    of the day's affairs
To all of my family
    gathered 'round there.

The witch it turns out
    was no witch at all,
But a lady from the next block,
    who gave Mom a call.

And the dragon was just
    some old machinery
At a construction site
    for the refinery.

The damsel and her
    kittycat in distress
Was the spoiled neighbor girl
    in a nice, little dress.

Later on, finally
    in bed for the night,
I pray and thank God
    for making me a knight,

For keeping me safe,
    for Divine protection,
And for family and friends,
    upon reflection.

Who knows what wonders
    tomorrow will hold,
More lands to be conquered
    by a knight so bold,

What galaxies await
    a space pioneer's trip --
A brave astronaut
    in his makeshift spaceship

Or the much anticipated maiden voyage
    of a mystery pirate with his faithful crew,
On a backyard ship decked out in black sails,
    sailing off to places only known to a few.

So come with me now
    on a different excursion,
Off to Mr. Sandman's
    nighttime aversions.

Places, times limited
    only by imagination
And a young boy
    or young girl's participation.

The past, the future,
    or even right now --
Whatever your conscious
    mind will allow.

Lose sight of what's real,
    and with me drift away
To another place,
    on another day!

Shopping with Reverend Spooner

I told my wife I was gonna go out,
    That I had to go to the store,
So she asked me to pick some stuff up --
    I didn't mind, so I told her, "Sure."

Lately she's been staying up reading,
    And it's starting to take it's toll.
Her words get all jumbled & tangled up,
    It's hard to talk to her, truth be told.

I've seen it up-close, seen it firsthand.
    It must be contagious -- it has to be.
I figure it spreads communicably,
    'Cause now it's happening to me...

~~~~~~~~~~~~~~~~~~~~~~

I said I'd go after I shook a tower,
    And grabbed a bite to eat.
I'd get some white chead and breese,
    And maybe some sandwich meat.

Or maybe I'd go to Kurger Bing,
    For a bamhurger and milk shake.
~~~~~~~~~~~~~~~~~~~~~~

Or DcMonald's for some Nicken McChuggets
    Or a McSausage Muffin with egg.

The neighbors had invited us over for chork pops,
    But for years now we've followed a dosher kiet.
We might have still went, and supped on their meal,
    But feared the worst -- a gastronomic riot.

When I got to the Mal-Wart,
    There were no sparking paces
But there was no shortage of signs
    with those blasted filey smaces.

There's only two items on my life's wist --
    A pack of dot hogs and hamburger buns
If I get the thong wring, she'll far & teather me,
    So I hope and pray I get the right ones!

When I got inside, a blushing crow I received.
    I find the right aisle where the products should be,
But as it urns tout, both were old sout,
    leaving the shelves bare and empty.

I stopped by the Mood Fart on my way home,
Got the lings on the thist, so everything
should be cool.
Except I forgot to get what I came for --
Some sandpaper and a pack of weel stool.

When I got home, my wife had supper waiting --
I could smell it from outside the door on the
stoop.
It's one of my favorites, that's for sure --
Chilled greese with a bowl of sea poop.

She's really enjoying the book that she's reading
--
"The Yoble Nuke of Dork and the Royal
Family"
She'd just finished one about Resident Pagan --
She loves history or a good biography.

She tells me good night, lost theep in dought,
Tharp as a shack and clever is she.
She's winding down, getting ready for bed,
With her cup of Teepy Slime tea.

And to the reader, I wish a good night,
Dreet sweams, and all that goes with it!
May might nares flee you, and bed bugs not bite,
And you be refreshed in body and in spirit!

Ode to Late Mornings

The early bird gets the worm,
or so you've heard it said,
But what about the poor worm,
who's left chewed up and dead?

But if it's really a bird
That you're longing to be,
Your best choice is the night owl --
Much wiser is he.

Or consider the mouse
who's first to the cheese --
It's the second mouse's
cheese, if you please.

Now if you go to bed early,
and you're early to rise,
Does it really leave you healthy,
wealthy, or wise?"

For few has it worked,
though many have tried.
It's just a bossman's mantra
to keep his workers on time.

Now if you want to come knockin',
    and not find me mean,
First pay heed to Proverbs,
    twenty-seven, fourteen.

Early this morning
    is just late last night,
And is it really morning
    if there isn't daylight?

If you stay up late enough,
    it stops being late,
And again becomes early,
    but with a new date.

Yesterday's tomorrow
    is tomorrow's yesterday,
But they're one and the same --
    they both are today.

Next time you consider
    setting an alarm,
And you think to yourself,
    "What's the harm?"

Just remember the worm
    at the first of this verse,
Then hope for better,
    but prepare for worse!

A Legacy Conjured

Some time long after
    you've breathed your last breath,
What would you have
    your tombstone to read?
Something to remember you
    after your death,
A personal motto
    or lifelong creed?

When people happen
    past your grave,
What message would you
    have them take away?
If you wrote it yourself
    for posterity,
Do you know what
    your obituary would say?

Now is the time
    to ponder these things,
Before you're
    dead and gone
Because then
    it will all be trusted
To those
    who yet live on.

Fill out a diary
    or notebook or journal,
Print off certificates
    and membership cards.
Hide them away
    in an old trunk or suitcase,
In the corner of an attic
    where they'll have to search hard.

So go ahead
    and write your own story,
And who better
    to do it than you?
Describe the person
    you wished you'd become,
Using photo apps --
    fix an image or two.

Award yourself a title
    or office or degree --
Doctor, Ph.D.,
    Reverend, or Lord,
Or maybe just change
    your middle initial,
After all,
    they're only just words.

Only words, yes, but then
    they could be so much more --
Remember being tasked
    with a family tree for school?
Consider your great,
    great, great grandkids
When they are trying hard
    to fit in and be cool --

Bragging rights
    not just for you,
But for generations
    to come.
They'll beam with pride
    whenever you're mentioned
And recount the deeds
    you've supposedly done.

Your memory will be
    larger than life --
Your descendants
    will surely be proud,
People you'll never
    even meet
Will sing your praises
    out loud.

Sure, genealogists
    will most likely despise you,
Some in vain
    will even take your name.
Others will curse
    the day you were born,
And your mother's
    good name defame.

But how could you ever
    assign a price
To the reputation
    you leave behind --
The legacy
    your progeny inherits,
And stories
    they'll one day find?

Vexation Embraced, or Plight of the Genealogist

Dark secrets laid buried
    in confusion and doubt --
From the closet long hidden,
    a skeleton peers out.
Marriages, trysts,
    and falsified ages,
Secrets surmised
    from long-faded pages,

Census and land grant,
    probated will,
Illegible texts
    penned by candle with quill.
Names and dates
    and places galore,
Every mystery left solved
    brings two mysteries more.

Descended from kings
    or begotten by wretches,
Legacies unfold
    in glimpses and sketches.
Engrossed by the content
    of dusty old tomes,

On a task neverending,
the undaunted plod on...

An Empty Page

The page sits before me,
  the poem not yet wrote.
Will it be contemplative
  or some anecdote?

A silly ballad
  or philosophical rhyme,
Limerick clever
  or joke set to time?

Each word carefully chosen,
  but not yet inked.
Segues selected
  so that stanzas be linked.

Meter gone over,
  checked time and again,
Each cadence just right,
  though yet to be penned.

The phrases go 'round
  and 'round in my head,
Vying for inclusion,
  that they might be read.

But ideas they are
    and not words that rhyme,
Although my grey matter's
    working overtime.

Some say it's writer's block --
    that's what they call it --
Like running a program
    before you install it.

But it's not writer's block
    that has me frustrated --
It's just that my muse,
    she's constipated.

The Chronomaster's Play

A cool, brisk breeze
    in the fall of the year --
A solemn reminder
    that winter draws near.

A lonesome owl calls
    on a dark, moonless night,
Assuring the forest
    that everything's alright.

The leaves have all turned,
    and have mostly fallen,
A harbinger that warns
    Jack Frost'll be calling,

Tangled tree limbs set
    against a purple sky,
The smell of smoke
    from a wood fire nearby.

These all set the stage
    for a performance so grand,
That the clouds seem to part,
    that Orion might attend.

The flames of a campfire
    dance in the dark night,
Mesmerizing those
    who watch its flickering light.

The crackling fire paints the quiet,
    sublime and profound,
Like darkness flees light,
    so the silence flees sound.

Wind whispers softly
    through dried leaves in the cold,
Telling a tale
    that's older than old.

Passing on secrets,
    some ancient, some new,
Heard by those worthy,
    and only those few,

The comings and goings
    of the forest all 'round,
Fill the night air with
    most harmonious sound.

The orchestra's assembled --
    howling wind, fire, and leaves,
Crying wolves distant,
    owls in the trees.

As the symphony of night
    plays eerily on,
The fading day prepares
    her final swan song.

As the day yields to night,
    then night to day again,
So the seasons turn,
    wheel and wheel within.

The cycle continues
    year by year, day to day,
For all who would come
    to the chronomaster's play.

State of Society

As a society, we
  progressively regress.
It's time that a few things
  be specifically addressed.

What once was bad,
  we now call good.
And what once was good
  is misunderstood.

Opposition to our
  law enforcement
Is nothing more than
  criminal endorsement.

Judging all for
  the misdeeds of a few
Shouldn't be done,
  but that's what some do.

Entertained by things
  that are quite immoral --
"But what about free speech,"
  some will quarrel,

But can we really
    say that it's free --
When it demeans
    and degrades society?

Condoning immorality
    leads to acceptance,
It's best destroyed
    while it still remains nascent.

Next it receives empathy
    then compassion in turn,
Until it's complacently embraced
    and naively seen as the norm.

Free sex and porn
    erode the family,
But again we mustn't
    mess with free speech.

Abortion that's used
    as birth control --
Legalized murder,
    of defenseless souls.

Take away the people's firearms --
    their most obvious way to defend
Against a corrupt and wicked regime,
    should they on the people decide to descend.

A government that fears
    its people with guns
Is a government to be feared,
    when the time comes.

War zones called schools
    breeding entitled youth.
Indoctrination machines
    devoid of truth.

Gender rebellion
    that leaves folks confused --
The perverts bemused,
    and the gullible abused.

Drug culture that brings
    hard drugs like a flood,
It's better stopped soon --
    nipped in the bud.

This list is just
    a sampling of sins,
Violations, and vices
    Committed by men.

When you boil it all down,
    the problem's not crime,
It's something you'll find
    that's much more sublime.

The problem began
    when we strayed into sin,
Left the Bible behind,
    forgot the lessons therein.

As Fortune Wills

What does it mean
    for a man to be king
And rule over
    his fellow beings?
Or a man who's a peasant,
    what keeps him in fetters,
Beneath those long
    considered his betters?

Born into poverty,
    born into privilege,
Being born
    to this world at all,
Who gets to decide
    all of these matters --
Who lives, who dies,
    who succeeds or falls?

Some work hard
    and claw their way up,
With perseverance
    and with patience
They attain all their hopes
    and achieve all their dreams,
To rise high
    above their stations.

Others work hard
    for all of their lives,
They seem
    to do everything right.
But never can they
    catch a break,
Though they struggle
    with all their might.

Just as the sun
    casts its light abroad,
And the wind blows
    where it will,
Fortune blesses
    as she sees fit,
Others she puts
    through the mill.

A fickle and carefree
    mistress is she.
She shares her affection
    with that one or this,
But take comfort in knowing
    that God's in control,
And He always takes care
    of those who are His.

On a whim fortune smiles
    or fortune neglects,
But it's only
    as God allows.
To trust Him in this
    takes a measure of faith,
But it surely must
    make Him proud!

Insatiable Us

What do we want
in the grand scheme of things?
Everyone seeks and yearns,
but what does all of it mean?

Never really are we satisfied,
are we?
Ever do we want more,
calling our wants our needs.
Enough is never enough,
though is it?
Do we dare to hope
to rise above our greed?

Yesterday we got by
with what we had then,
And today we get by
on what we have again.
How can we expect to do
tomorrow as much as today?
We must have more now,
if we're to win.
Even if we had enough
to satisfy our needs,
How could wanting more
possibly be a sin?

Contemplation of Life by Man

If wrong is determined by that which is right,
And right by One greater than me,
Which right is righter and wrong is worse
Of all the rights that could be?

Truth stands alone, without our approval,
Agreement, blessing, or consent.
It matters little what end they affect --
Our purposes, our wills, our intents.

To venture a thought or ponder aloud
The origin of our morals
Is to consider the very nature of God
And His will for us mere mortals.

Be they right or wrong or a little of both,
Our actions define who we are --
Actions that are driven by our beliefs,
Reflections of what's in our hearts.

Our treatment of others, our feelings toward
God,
Our thoughts about life after death --
These are the things that color our lives
And determine what we like or detest.

Through this life we make our way,
Though we're promised not even a grave.
What we leave behind is the legacy
That we're building day by day.

Our memories live on in the deeds that we've done
In the memories of those left behind.
What's right or wrong with the lives that we lead
Others in their minds will decide.

So in the end, when the day is done,
And we've lived as best we can,
While our earthly bodies return to the dust,
Our real lives we just began.

A Sojourner's Lessons

I made it back to my home last night
After too many days & too many nights.
The people I knew were all strangers again,
What used to be family and used to be friends.

I've been down the road and back again,
And I've learned to embrace time as my friend.
Make each day count, learn to take it slow,
'Cause you go to sleep young, & you wake up
old.

I've seen a poor man standing as tall as a king,
And a rich man fall in shame to his knees.
The strong grow old, and the young grow strong,
The hourglass turns, and it doesn't take long.

I couldn't tell you of all the places I've been,
The people I've met, or the things that I did.
You wake up, live a day, sleep again,
Life goes by like a whisper in the wind.

The Author's Gratitude

THANK YOU, dear reader, for taking the time
To share a small part of my life!
I hope that I've left you with at least a smile,
In this world full of chaos and strife.

What began as a challenge to write a few poems
Has uncovered a passion that's been long asleep,
Lying dormant and waiting for just the right time
To prove itself worthy, a hobby to keep.

Amazing how quickly the hourglass has drained!
Our time has come and went too fast.
I'm sure more verses are yet to be written,
Before all of the dice are cast.

So 'til then fill your days with joy and laughter,
And may each one be better than the one just
passed.
Go live your God-given life to the fullest,
And make the kind of memories that last.

It looks like we've finally come to the end,
So 'til next time, I bid you, "Adieu!"
I wish you and yours all of the best --
And again, in all caps, I say, "THANK YOU!!"

www.ingramcontent.com/pod-product-compliance
Lightning Source LLC
Chambersburg PA
CBHW051733130826
49812CB00033B/846
9789357212540